A REASON FOR WRITING

ITION

"WORDS OF JESUS"

This book belongs to:

A Concerned Communications Publication

authors: Carol Ann Retzer and Eva Hoshino
senior editor: Bill Morelan
copy editor: Patricia Horning Benton
cover design: Daniel Potter
cover illustration: Mary Bausman
illustrations: Mark Ford
inside design: Walt Woesner
Scripture border sheets: Rita Hoshino and Sarah Thurstenson

For more information about A REASON FOR WRITING®, write or call:
Concerned Communications
P.O. Box 1000
Siloam Springs, Arkansas 72761
Telephone (501) 549-9000

©1984, 1991, 1998 by Concerned Communications. All rights reserved.
No material in this series may be reproduced in any form
without written permission from the publisher.
Printed in U.S.A.

Verses marked TLB are taken fron *The Living Bible*, ©1971
by Tyndale House Publishers, Wheaton, Illinois. Used by permission.
To be consistent with the traditional form in reference to God, pronouns referring to God are capitalized
To shorten verses to the age level of first and second graders, in some instances words
which do not change the meaning of the text have been omitted.

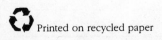
Printed on recycled paper

Hello Friend!

We're Sarah, Rob, Ginny, and Calvin. You'll see more of us in the next few weeks.

We needed help when we first started to write. Now we want to help you!

We formed our Golden Rule Club to help other kids. Won't you join us? Together we can work on handwriting. We'll also learn how to be better Christians.

You'll see members of our Golden Rule Club at the top of each verse lesson. We'll share handwriting tips as well as ways to be better friends to each other. Good handwriting takes practice. Being a good friend takes practice too.

Do your best as you practice the letters, words, and verses in the lessons ahead. You will find a review of manuscript letters (pages 9 - 20). Remember to write each letter on the line and fill the space to make it easier to read.

Printing is a skill that you will need all through your life. You will soon be writing in cursive but printing will always be helpful to you.

You will write the verse of the week on a border sheet and decorate it weekly. One way you can be a member of the Golden Rule Club is to find some way to share the verse. Many students are sharing verses with neighbors, shut-ins, family members, church members, and senior citizens. People who have received the verses have been blessed by the message and by being remembered. Let us know if you find more ways to share your verses.

The Bible tells us to treat other people the way we want to be treated. That is following the Golden Rule. Members of the Golden Rule Club promise to help other people. We hope you'll join the club and find someone to help each day.

Your friends for better writing,

The Golden Rule Club

The Golden Rule Club's Tips for Better Writing

✎ **Hold your pencil correctly. Slant your paper in the right direction. (See the pictures on page 5.)**

✎ **Sit up straight, with your feet flat on the floor.**

✎ **Form each letter the right way.**

✎ **Space nicely between each letter and word. Your finger can be your guide. Put the finger next to your thumb between words. Doesn't that amount of space look nice in the picture?**

✎ **Take time to make each letter carefully.**

Proper Hand and Paper Position

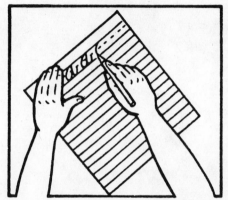

Right-handed

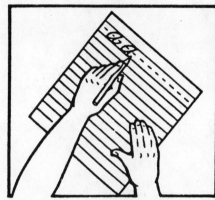

Left-handed

Correct Manuscript Formation of Letters and Numbers

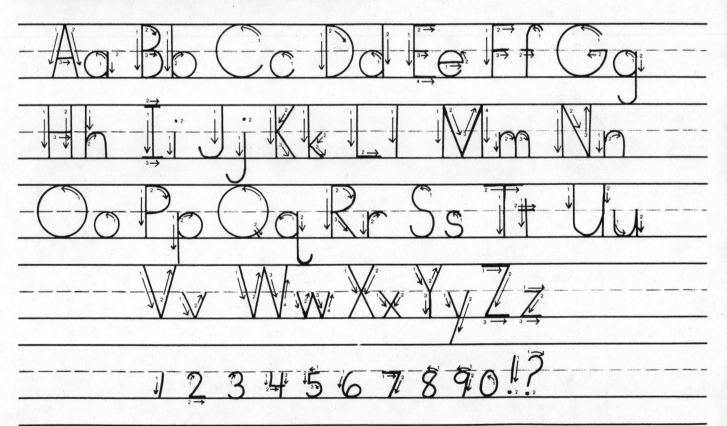

PRACTICE PAGES

MANUSCRIPT →

A Reason For Writing

1

NAME

a b c d e f g h i

j k l m n o p q

r s t u v w x y z

9

NAME

c

o

a

d

g

e

3

m   m

n   n

h   h

i   i

t   t

l   l

NAME

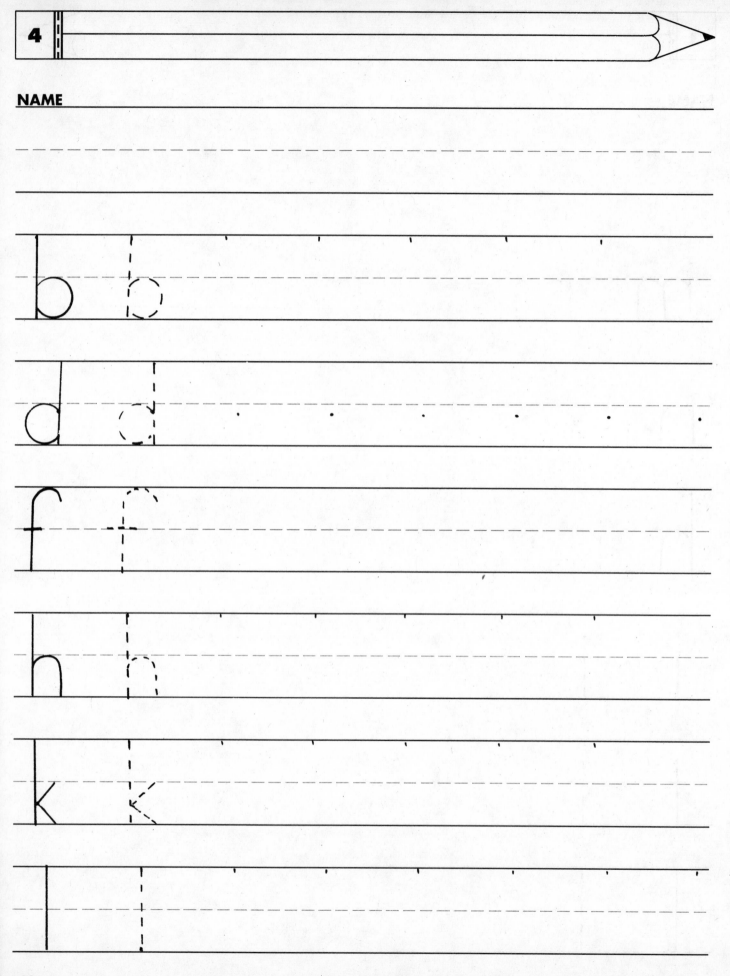

NAME

h h

m m

n n

r r

u u

s s

NAME

g g

j j

p p

g g

y y

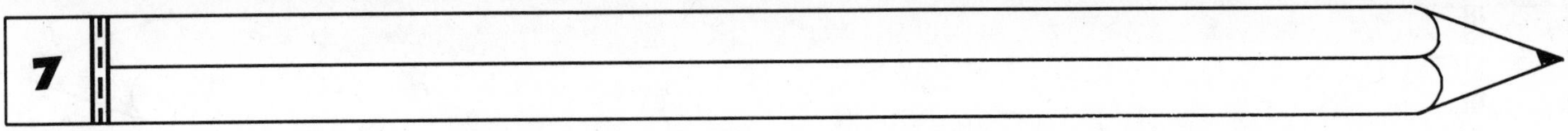

NAME

K k

V v

W w

X x

Y y

Z z

8

0

1

2

3

4

NAME

5

6

7

8

9

NAME

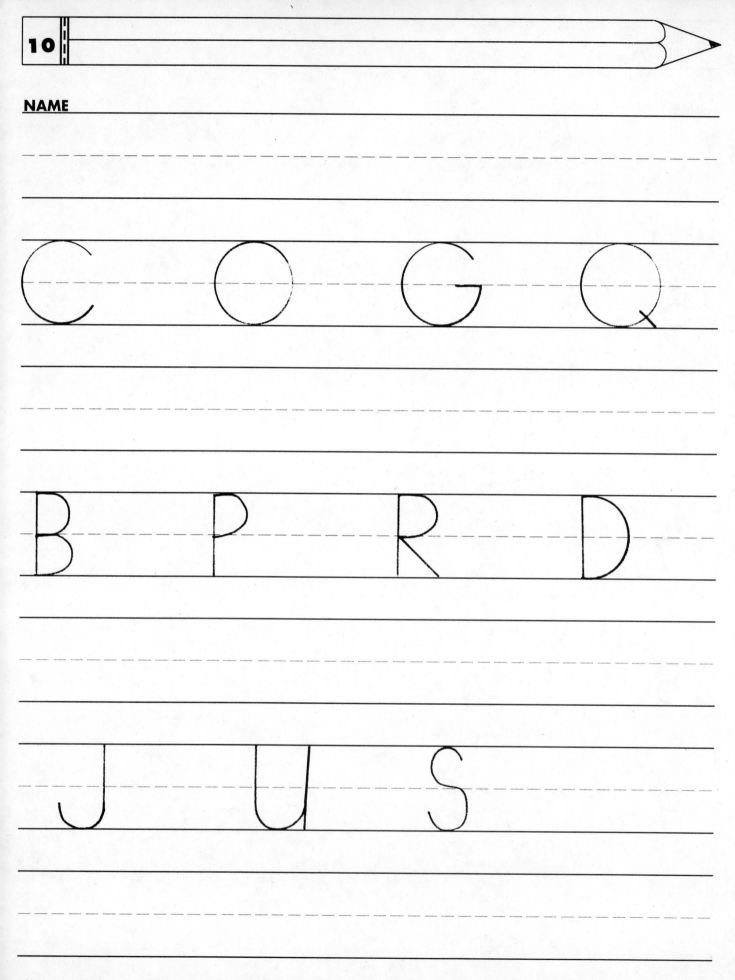

C O G Q

B P R D

J U S

NAME

E F H I L

T K M N V

A W X Y Z

12

NAME

WEEKLY LESSONS

MANUSCRIPT →

A Reason For Writing

LESSON 1

Let's practice the a and the d this week.

Make these letters starting at the 2 o'clock position. Don't pick up your pencil until you've finished the letter.

DAY 1

a

d

DAY 2

all

and

heart

mind

Lord

God

VERSE OF THE WEEK

"Love the Lord
your God with all
your heart, soul, and
mind."
Matt. 22:37

LESSON 2

Some people always want to be first.

This verse tells us how to be *great*.

DAY 1

g

o

DAY 2

for

others

of

go

great

give

VERSE OF THE WEEK

"Your care for others
is the measure of
your greatness."

Luke 9:48

26

LESSON 3

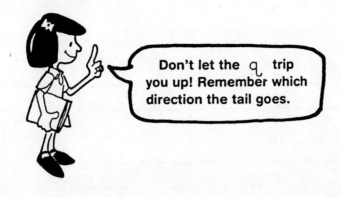

Don't let the q trip you up! Remember which direction the tail goes.

DAY 1

q

a

DAY 2

to

too

it

is

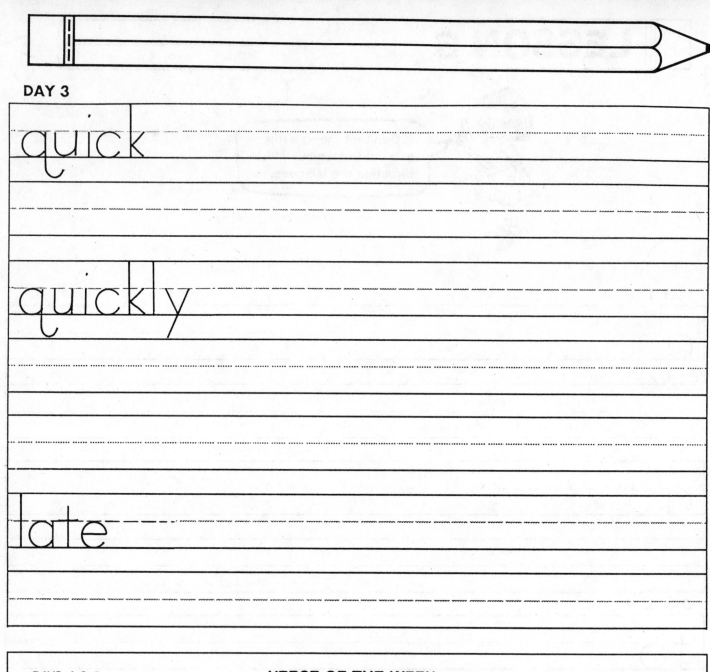

DAY 3

quick

quickly

late

DAYS 4 & 5   **VERSE OF THE WEEK**

"Come to terms
quickly before it is
too late."

Matt. 5:25

28

LESSON 4

Work on the c and e this week.

Golden Rule Club members can help share peace. Think of how you can live in peace this week.

DAY 1

c

e

DAY 2

peace

each

live

DAY 3

other

in

with

DAYS 4 & 5   **VERSE OF THE WEEK**

"Live in peace with each other."

Mark 9:50

LESSON 5

Don't be fooled by these two letters— b and p . They look similar, but each is different.

DAY 1

b

p

DAY 2

be

big

book

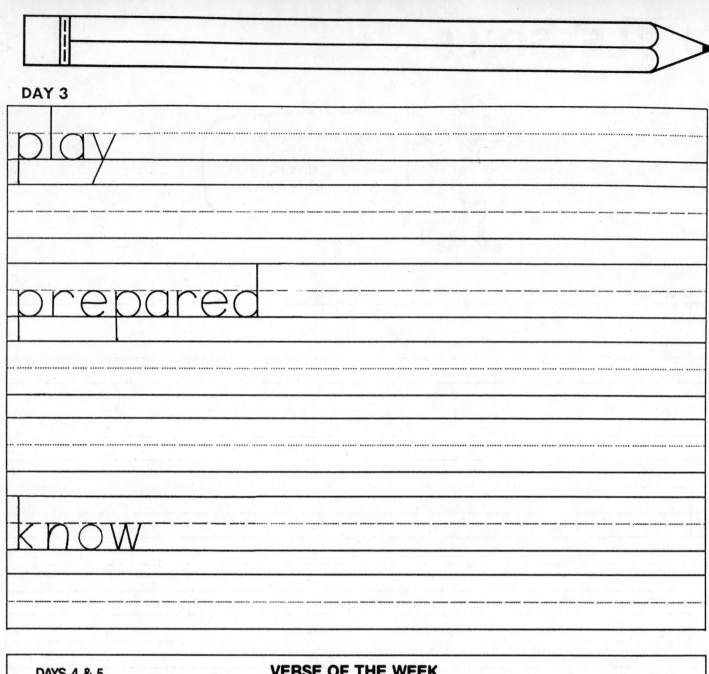

DAY 3

play

prepared

know

DAYS 4 & 5   **VERSE OF THE WEEK**

"Be prepared, for you don't know what day your Lord is coming."

Matt. 24:42

TLB

LESSON 6

Watch the starting place for the i , the † , and the | .

Another word for *disciple* is *learner*. I guess that makes us all disciples.

DAY 1

i

†

|

DAY 2

the

that

then

love

will

world

VERSE OF THE WEEK

"Your strong love for each other will prove to the world that you are my disciples."

John 13:35

TLB

LESSON 7

Our practice letters this week are similar— h , n , m , r .

But only one of them starts at the roof. Circle the letter that starts there.

DAY 1

h

n

m

r

DAY 2

home

has

what

DAY 3

things

them

done

VERSE OF THE WEEK

"Go home to your friends, and tell them what wonderful things God has done for you."

Mark 5:19

TLB

LESSON 8

Both practice letters f and † are crossed *after* the down stroke is finished.

The light in this week's verse is one your mom won't tell you to turn off!

DAY 1

f

†

DAY 2

fill

face

if

you

are

light

VERSE OF THE WEEK

"If you are filled

with light within, then

your face will be

radiant too."

Luke 11:36

TLB

LESSON 9

The j and the i are very much alike, except one has a curved tail.

Think of things that make you joyful. Rejoice in Jesus' love!

DAY 1

j

i

DAY 2

jump

rejoice

joy

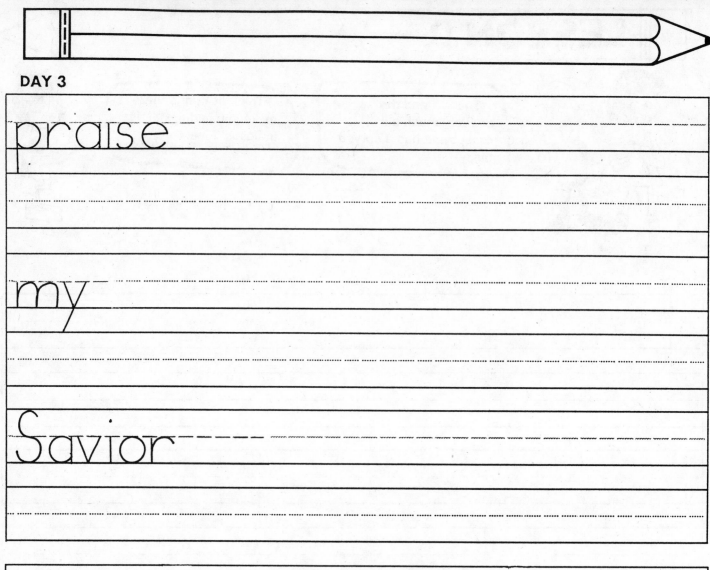

DAY 3

praise

my

Savior

DAYS 4 & 5   **VERSE OF THE WEEK**

"Oh, how I praise
the Lord. How I rejoice
in God my Savior!"

Luke 1: 46, 47

TLB

LESSON 10

Both the u and the v are made without lifting your pencil. Practice making nice, smooth strokes.

DAY 1

u

v

DAY 2

your

much

love

as

up

us

use

"Love your neighbor as much as you love yourself."

Matt. 22:39

LESSON 11

The y is one letter made with two strokes. Pick up your pencil before you make the long tail.

Isn't it good that some things never change? Think of something else in the Bible that is always the same.

DAY 1

W

y

DAY 2

away

words

yet

43

heaven

true

shall

VERSE OF THE WEEK

"Though all heaven
and earth shall pass
away, yet My words
remain forever true."

Luke 21:33

44

TLB

LESSON 12

The x has two strokes the same length.

Keep your pencil going in one smooth stroke for the letter s .

DAY 1

x

s

DAY 2

exist

exit

six

45

said

didn't

make

VERSE OF THE WEEK

"He created every-
thing there is — nothing
exists that He didn't
make."

John 1:3

TLB

LESSON 13

The k and the h both begin in the roof. One of these letters is made with one stroke. The other has two. Draw a box around the letter with two strokes.

DAY 1

k

h

DAY 2

take

keep

kind

cross

his

know

VERSE OF THE WEEK

"If anyone wants to be a follower of mine, let him take up his cross and follow Me."

Matt. 16:24

TLB

LESSON 14

This verse reminds me of something from Australia. What is it that returns to the person who throws it?

DAY 1

z

b

DAY 2

buzz

never

or

come

on

criticize

"Never criticize or
condemn—or it will
all come back on you."

Luke 6:37

TLB

LESSON 15

Do these pairs of letters look like parents and children? The lowercase letters are exactly like the capitals, except they're smaller.

DAY 1

Cc

Oo

DAY 2

came

truth

who

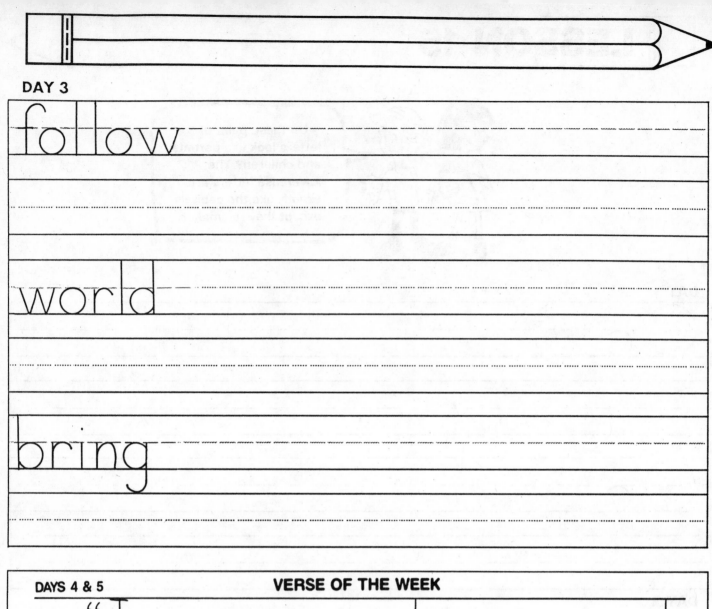

DAY 3

follow

world

bring

DAYS 4 & 5   **VERSE OF THE WEEK**

"I came to bring truth
to the world. All who
love the truth are
My followers."

John 18:37

TLB

LESSON 16

Who are you going to share your verse with this week, Ginny?

DAY 1

Ss

Ww

DAY 2

worship

We

so

say

Scriptures

must

VERSE OF THE WEEK

"We must worship

God, and Him alone.

So it is written in the

Scriptures."

Luke 4:8

LESSON 17

Here are two lowercase letters that *don't* look like their capitals. Circle the pair that are made with the same stroke.

DAY 1

Pp

Hh

Ee

DAY 2

Praise

people

them

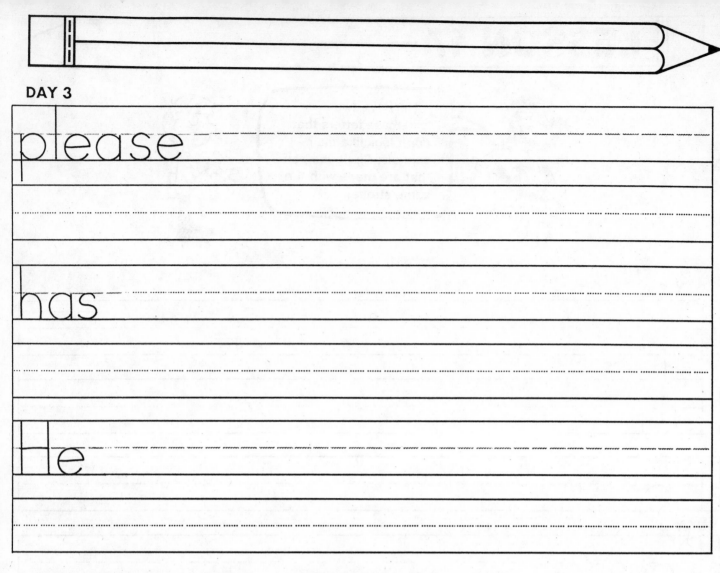

DAY 3

please

has

He

DAYS 4 & 5 **VERSE OF THE WEEK**

"Praise the Lord, for He has come to visit His people and has redeemed them."

Luke 1:68

TLB

LESSON 18

The practice letters this week are look-alikes. See how straight you can make all the strokes.

DAY 1

Vv

Xx

DAY 2

even

always

end

am

with

world

VERSE OF THE WEEK

"I am with you always, even to the end of the world."

Matt. 28:20

TLB

LESSON 19

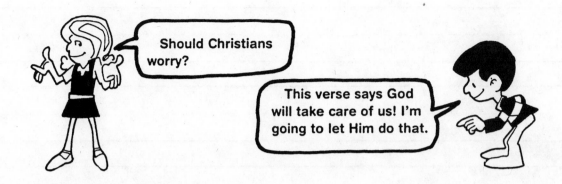

Should Christians worry?

This verse says God will take care of us! I'm going to let Him do that.

DAY 1

I

Zz

DAY 2

care

time

day

DAY 3

at

prize

tomorrow

VERSE OF THE WEEK

"God will take care
of your tomorrow. Live
one day at a time."
Matt. 6:34
TLB

LESSON 20

Remember that the
† is the one letter that
begins in the middle of
the space.

It's a letter I write a
lot. I'll practice it today
and tomorrow.

DAY 1

Tt

Gg

DAY 2

there

angels

the

when

repent

in

VERSE OF THE WEEK

"There is joy in the presence of the angels of God when one sinner repents."

Luke 15:10

TLB

LESSON 21

Let's review some letters we've learned.

We can practice our letters and our listening this week.

DAY 1

Ee

Pp

DAY 2

ears

listen

sure

put

hear

practice

"If you have ears,
listen! Be sure to put
into practice what you
hear."

Mark 4:23,24

LESSON 22

Watch for two words that sound alike but are spelled differently. Can you find them in this week's practice?

DAY 1

Ff

Hh

Yy

DAY 2

Father

for

four

65

Holy

Your

ask

VERSE OF THE WEEK

"Your heavenly Father

will give the Holy Spirit

to those who ask for

Him."

Luke 11:13

TLB

One of these lowercase letters is very different from its capital. After you write your practice letters, circle the different pair.

DAY 1

Bb

Cc

Gg

DAY 2

Bless

Word

into

DAY 3

can

guess

God

VERSE OF THE WEEK

"Blessed are all who hear the Word of God and put it into practice"

Luke 11:28

TLB

Would you like to discover a gold mine? Then memorize the Verse of the Week!

You'll be rich if you follow the message of this verse.

DAY 1

Dd

Aa

DAY 2

Do

what

want

DAY 3

them

down

you

DAYS 4 & 5   **VERSE OF THE WEEK**

"Do for others what

you want them to do

for you."

Matt. 7:12

TLB

LESSON 25

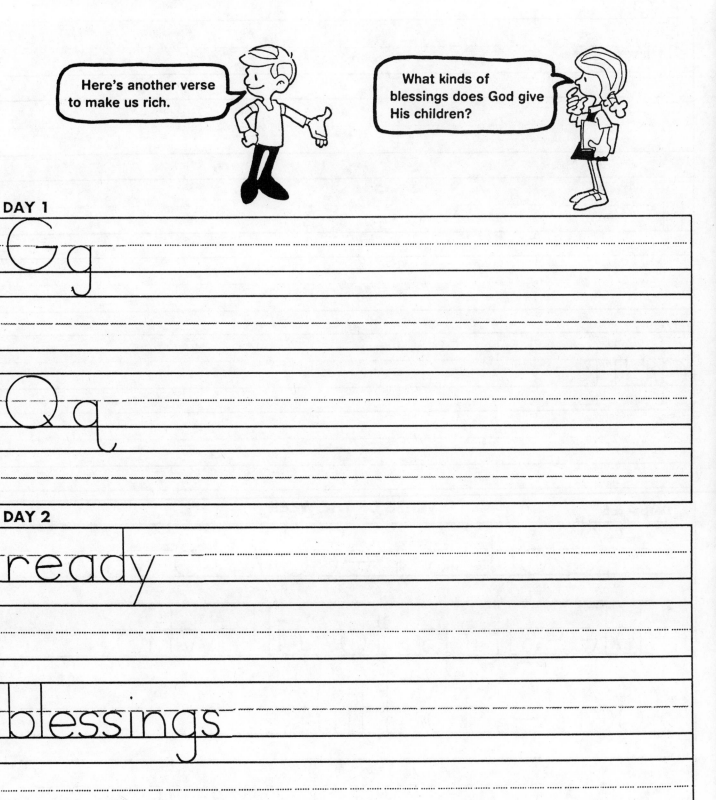

Here's another verse to make us rich.

What kinds of blessings does God give His children?

DAY 1

Gg

Qq

DAY 2

ready

blessings

all

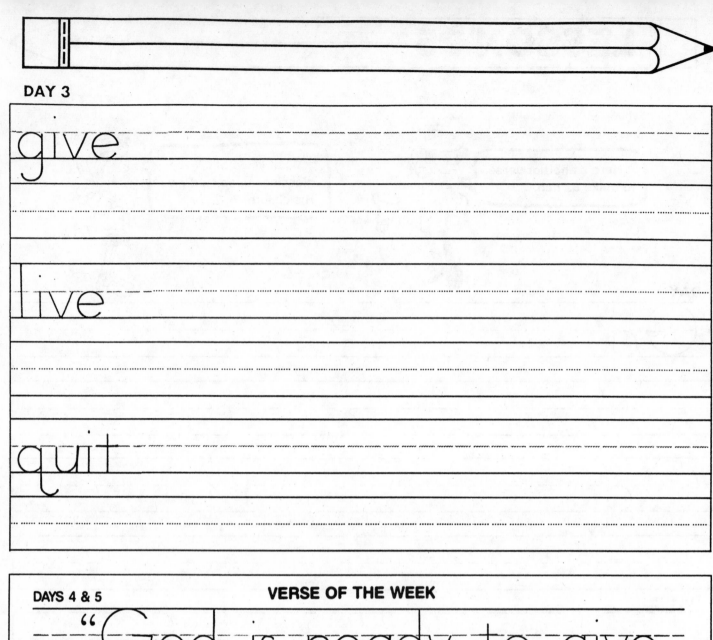

give

live

quit

"God is ready to give blessings to all who come to Him."

Luke 4:19

TLB

LESSON 26

How does truth set people free?

What kinds of things do we need to be set free from?

DAY 1

Yy

Ee

DAY 2

You

yes

ever

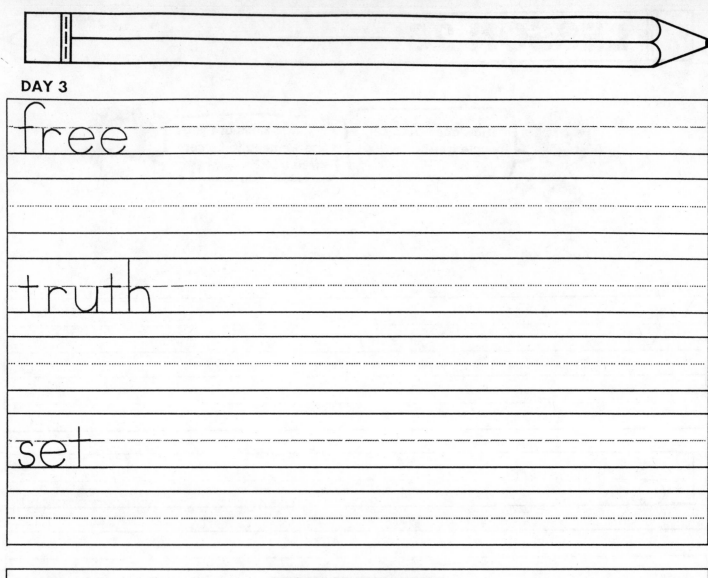

DAY 3

free

truth

set

DAYS 4 & 5 **VERSE OF THE WEEK**

"You will know the truth, and the truth will set you free."

John 8:32

TLB

Christians should be friendly. I'm going to try to make a new friend this week.

DAY 1

M m

F f

DAY 2

from

friend

only

DAY 3

friendly

different

If

?

DAYS 4 & 5   **VERSE OF THE WEEK**

"If you are friendly
only to your friends,
how are you different
from anyone else?"

Matt. 5:47

LESSON 28

Sometimes we need to turn our backs on something.

Sometimes we need to turn our faces toward something better.

DAY 1

Kk

Ii

Nn

DAY 2

Turn

sin

near

DAY 3

Kingdom

I

keep

VERSE OF THE WEEK

"Turn from sin, and turn to God, for the Kingdom of heaven is near."

Matt. 4:17

78   TLB

LESSON 29

What's another word for *return*?

I know! I'm waiting for Jesus' Second *Coming*!

DAY 1

J j

R r

DAY 2

joy

wait

ready

DAY 3

return

rich

jump

VERSE OF THE WEEK

"There will be great joy for those who are ready and waiting for His return."

Luke 12:37

80

TLB

LESSON 30

Jesus wants His friends to be honest about everything.

Is there anything too small to be honest about?

DAY 1

Uu

Nn

Tt

DAY 2

Unless

honest

won't

small

large

matters

"Unless you are honest in small matters, you won't be in large ones."

Luke 16:10

TLB

TRANSITION SECTION

To The Teacher:

This section has been added for classroom teachers who feel their students are ready to begin transition to cursive in the second half of grade 2.

You may use as much or as little of this section as you need.

A Reason For Writing

Write Right Two Ways

Most kids can't wait to write cursive! It's fun to write like an adult. It's also faster to write in cursive.

This section will help you learn to master cursive writing. You will enjoy learning the new strokes and letters. Within a few weeks you will be able to write a whole page in cursive.

But don't forget manuscript writing! Right now you may think you will never use manuscript writing again. But once in a while you will. Can you think of a time when your parents use manuscript writing?

Maybe you've seen your mother addressing a package to mail. Did she write the label in manuscript? Have you watched your dad filling out a form for a credit card? He probably used manuscript.

This section will help you to learn cursive writing step-by-step. Soon it will be easy!

But don't forget how to make good, clear manuscript letters. You'll need that skill your whole life.

Remember to write both ways!

Tips for Checking Your Cursive Writing

Look at a page of your cursive handwriting. Then see how your paper measures up in these areas:

✏️ **Formation:** Is each letter formed correctly? Look at the chart if you can't remember how to make a cursive letter. Remember to write a complete word without lifting your pencil!

✏️ **Spacing:** Are the letters in each word spaced evenly? Is there more space between words?

✏️ **Slant:** Do the letters slant slightly forward without falling over? The slant should be uniform. (If you are left-handed, you may have to work harder for a good slant.)

✏️ **Capitals:** Does each sentence begin with a capital letter? Are proper names also capitalized? Is each capital letter a full space tall?

✏️ **Punctuation:** Does each sentence end with the correct punctuation mark?

✏️ **Numbers:** Does each number come only to the dotted line?

✏️ **Readability:** Finally, is your handwriting easy to read? If you were careful to do your best in all the areas above, the answer should be Yes! People will give you high marks for handwriting that can be read easily.

Correct Cursive Formation of Letters and Numbers

Aa Bb Cc Dd Ee

Ff Gg Hh Ii Jj

Kk Ll Mm Nn Oo

Pp Qq Rr Ss Tt

Uu Vv Ww Xx Yy

Zz

1 2 3 4 5 6 7 8 9 10

* NOTE TO STUDENTS

Notice how each manuscript and cursive letter is alike and how they are different.

If you have been making most of your manuscript letters with <u>one stroke</u> you will easily make the transition to cursive writing.

Follow the arrows to begin each cursive letter correctly.

Your writing shares your words with others.

Happy writing to you in the days ahead.

PRACTICE PAGES

TRANSITION →

A Reason For Writing

1

NAME

Aa *Aa Aa*

a a

a

a

aaa aaa

aaa

A

A

A

A

NAME

E e E l E e

l e

e

e

l l l

l e e

E

e

e

e

NAME

$I i$ li iii

i

i

i

iii

iii

l

l

l

l

4

NAME

O o O o O o

o o

o

o

o o o

o o o

O

O

O

O

94

NAME

𝒰 𝓊 𝒰 𝓊 𝓊 𝒰𝓊

𝓊 𝓊

𝓊

𝓊

𝓊𝓊𝓊𝓊𝓊

𝓊𝓊𝓊𝓊𝓊

𝒰

𝒰

𝒰

𝒰

NAME

l

e

i

i

u

u

a

a

o

o

NAME

C c C c C c

C c

c

c

ccc

ccc

C

C

C

C

NAME

D d *Dd Dd*

d d

d

d

ddd

ddd

D

D

D

D

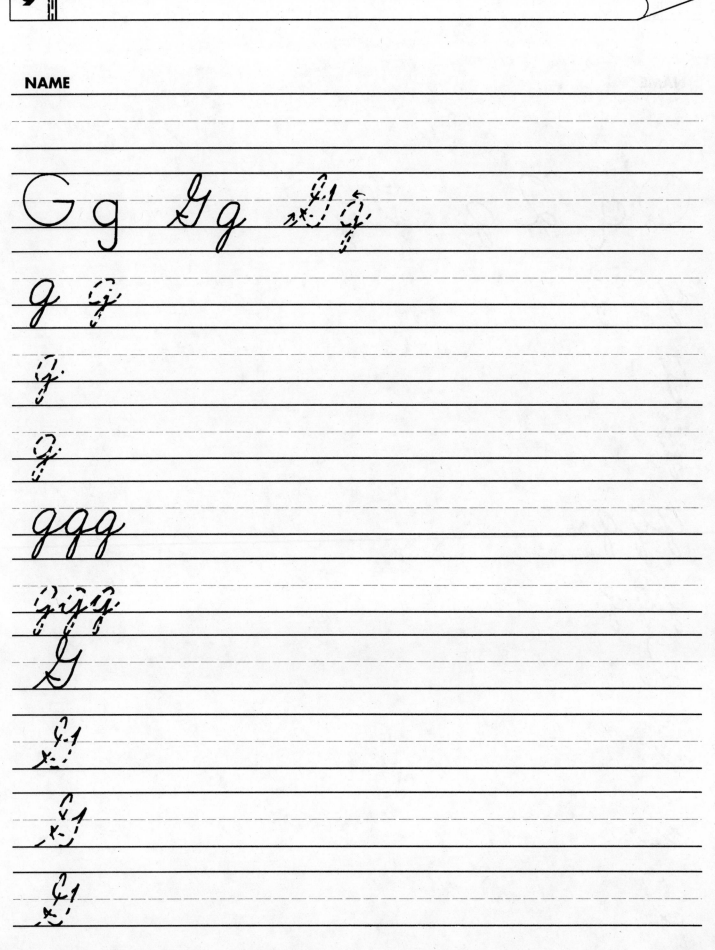

NAME

NAME

Q q 2 q 2 q

q q

q

q

q q q

q q q

2

2

2

2

NAME

Hh *Hh* *Hh*

h h

h

h

hhh

hhh

H

H

H

H

NAME

L l L l L l

l l

l

l

lll

lll

L

L

L

L

NAME

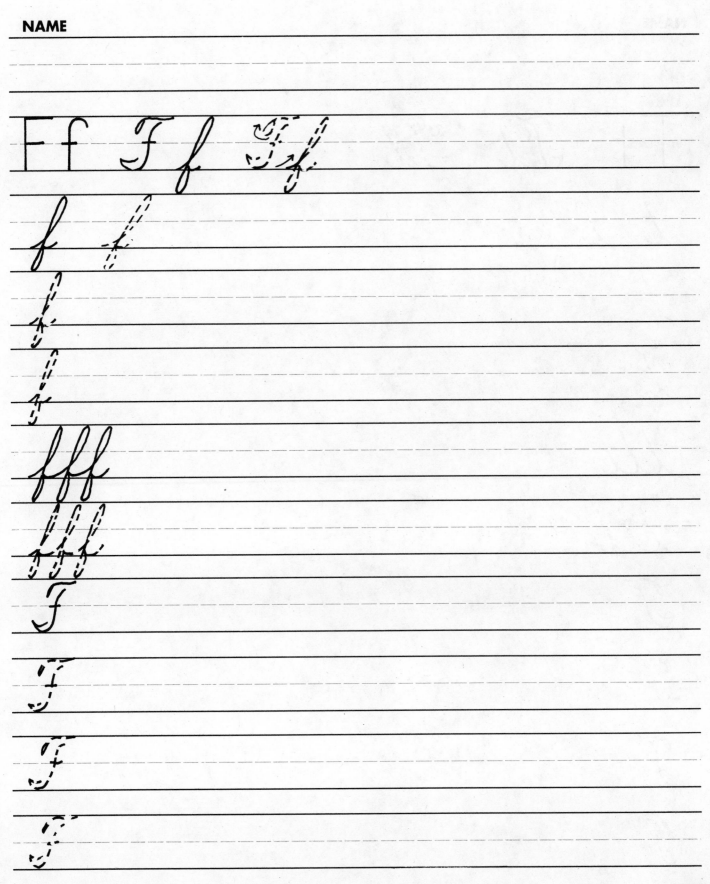

NAME

T t T t T t

t t

t

t

ttt

ttt

T

T

T

T

NAME

c

d

g

q

h

l

f

t

had

let

16

NAME

Kk *Kk* *Kk*

k k

k

k

kkk

kkk

K

K

K

K

NAME

Bb Bb Bb

b b

b

b

bbb

bbb

B

B

B

B

NAME

Ww Ww Ww

w w

w

w

www

$w\text{-}w\text{-}w$

W

W

W

W

NAME

P p P p P p

p p

p

p

p p p

p p p

P

P

P

P

NAME

J j f j j j

j j

j

j

j j j

j j j

f

f

f

NAME

Rr Rr Rr

R R

R

R

rrr

rrr

R

R

R

R

NAME

S s Ss Ss

S s

s

s

sss

sss

S

S

S

S

23

k

b

w

p

j

r

s

was

put

are

24

NAME

M m *M m M m*

m m

m

m

mmm

mmm

M

M

M

M

25

NAME

N n 𝒩 𝓃 𝒩 𝓃

𝓃 𝓃

𝓃

𝓃

𝓃𝓃𝓃

𝓃𝓃𝓃

𝒩

𝒩

𝒩

𝒩

26

NAME

V v Vv Vv

v v

v

v

vvv

vvv

V

V

V

V

NAME

$\mathcal{X}$ x $\mathcal{X}$ α

α

α

$\alpha\alpha\alpha$

NAME

Y y Y y Y y

Y y

y

y

y y y

y y y

Y

y

y

y

NAME

Zz *Zz Zz*

NAME

m

n

v

x

y

z

very

yes

zoo

man

NAME

NAME

e   l   b   h   k   f

i   u   j   w   s   r   t

n   m   y   v   x   z

a   d   g   q   o   c

p   q   j   y   z   f

33

NAME

a b c d e f g h i j k

l m n o p q r s t u

v w x y z

NAME

H K M N W

X U V Y L Z

B I G S F T

O C E A D

J L P R

35

NAME

A B C D E F G H

I J K L M N O P

Q R S T U V W X

Y Z

NAME

ba

bl

wi

wo

vi

NAME

va

od

or

ir

er

NAME

ph

gh

ju

sp

gs

NAME

at

and

the

you

to

NAME

of

be

in

we

I

41

NAME

NAME

God

made

the

animals

God made the animals.

43

NAME

Be

kind

to

your

neighbor

Be kind to your neighbor.

44

NAME

Can

I

help

you

Can I help you?

45

NAME

Please

help

your

friend

Please help your friend.

46

NAME

Give

a

big

smile

away

Give a big smile away.

NAME

Matthew

Mark

Luke

John

Gospels

NAME

Aa Bb Cc Dd Ee Ff

Gg Hh Ii Jj Kk

Ll Mm Nn Oo Pp

Qq Rr Ss Tt Uu Vv

Ww Xx Yy Zz

WEEKLY LESSONS

TRANSITION →

A Reason For Writing

You Are Ready for Cursive Lessons!

You are ready to begin writing whole pages in cursive writing. Each week you will practice writing one verse from the New Testament. Do you know how some of the New Testament books were written?

Three days each week you will practice writing words from the Verse of the Week. By Thursday you will be ready to practice the whole verse. On Friday you can write it on a pretty Scripture border sheet. After you have decorated the page, you can share it with someone else.

Enjoy writing each one of these verses. Memorize as many as you can. And remember to share Scripture with others as often as possible!

For the rest of the year you'll be doing verse lessons in this book. Here is what you will do each week:

Weekly Schedule

Day 1

Read the handwriting tip at the first of the lesson. Then carefully practice the letters and words for the day.

Day 2

You'll have new letters and words from the Verse of the Week to practice today in this book.

Day 3

Review the handwriting tip. Make sure you're forming letters and words correctly as you practice. After you've finished practicing, take a moment to look back over the whole lesson to see how your handwriting measures up against the model.

Day 4

Write the verse on practice paper at least once. If you have time, start coloring the Scripture border sheet you'll finish tomorrow.

Day 5

In your best handwriting, write the Verse of the Week on your Scripture border sheet. Finish decorating the border. Think of someone who would enjoy your beautiful verse. Smile as you give it to that person.

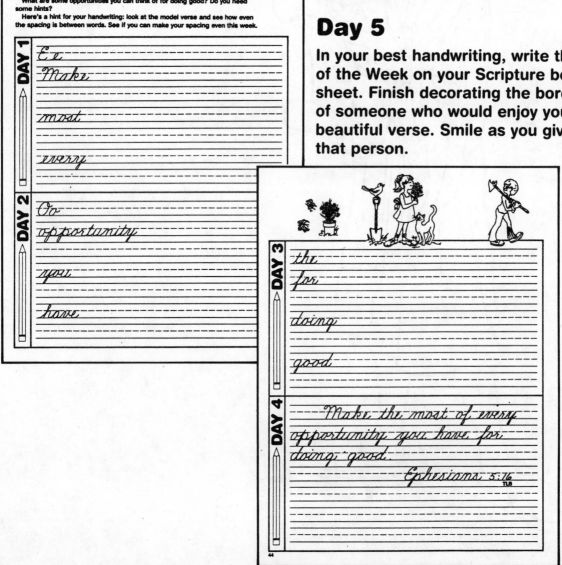

LESSON 1

There are lots of capitals to practice this week. Notice that capitals start in different places. Be sure to begin each one correctly.

DAY 1

Ee

Pp

Ii

DAY 2

ears

listen

sure

put

practice

hear

VERSE OF THE WEEK

If you have ears, listen! Be sure to put into practice what you hear.

Mark 4:23, 24

LESSON 2

Look at the dotted line. Are your short letters stopping at that point?

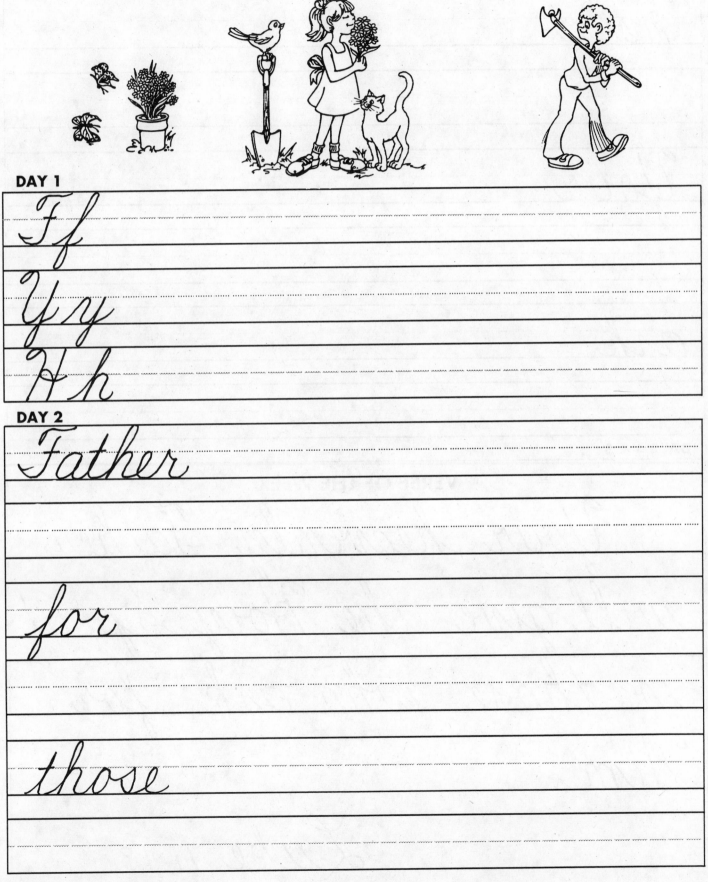

DAY 1

Ff

Yy

Hh

DAY 2

Father

for

those

Holy

Your

ask

VERSE OF THE WEEK

Your heavenly Father
will give the Holy Spirit
to those who ask for
Him.

Luke 11:13

LESSON 3

Here's a hint for your handwriting: look at the model verse and see how even the spacing is between words. See if you can make your spacing even this week.

DAY 1

Bb

Gg

Cc

DAY 2

Bless

Word

into

DAY 3

guess

God

who

can

DAYS 4 & 5

VERSE OF THE WEEK

Blessed are all who
hear the Word of God
and put it into practice.
Luke 11:28

LESSON 4

Look carefully at the model. How tall are the numbers? Make sure that **all** the numbers you write this week end at the middle line.

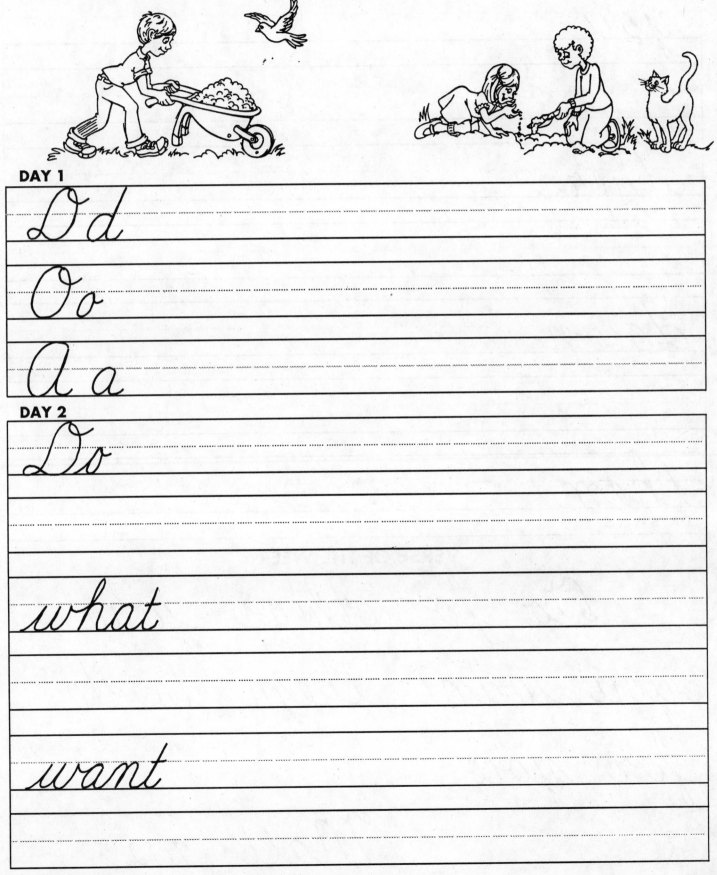

DAY 1

Dd

Oo

Aa

DAY 2

Do

what

want

you

others

down

them

VERSE OF THE WEEK

Do for others what
you want them to do
for you.

Matt. 7:12

LESSON 5

Look at your handwriting critically this week. Is each letter formed correctly? Is there enough space between words? Is the slant uniform? Is the page easy to read?

DAY 1

Q q

Z z

G g

DAY 2

ready

blessings

all

DAY 3

give

quit

live

Him

DAYS 4 & 5

VERSE OF THE WEEK

God is ready to give
blessings to all who
come to Him.

Luke 4:19

LESSON 6

Watch the letters with tails this week. The tail should barely touch the top of the next line.

DAY 1

Yy

Ss

Ee

DAY 2

You

know

ever

DAY 3

free

truth

set

DAYS 4 & 5

VERSE OF THE WEEK

You will know the truth, and the truth will set you free.

John 8:32

154

LESSON 7

Can you count the members in God's family? Isn't it fun to have so many brothers and sisters?

DAY 1

M m

F f

X x

DAY 2

friend

only

else

friendly

different

Li

?

VERSE OF THE WEEK

If you are friendly only to your friends, how are you different from anyone else?

Matt. 5:47

LESSON 8

Think of at least one good, kind thing you can do today. Can you help someone at home? Does another student in your class need your help?

DAY 1

$\mathcal{K}\,k$

$\mathcal{L}\,i$

$\mathcal{N}\,n$

DAY 2

$Turn$

$near$

sin

DAY 3

Kingdom

heaven

keep

DAYS 4 & 5

VERSE OF THE WEEK

Turn from sin, and
turn to God, for the
Kingdom of heaven is
near.

Matt. 4:17

BORDER
SHEETS

MANUSCRIPT $\longrightarrow$

A Reason For Writing

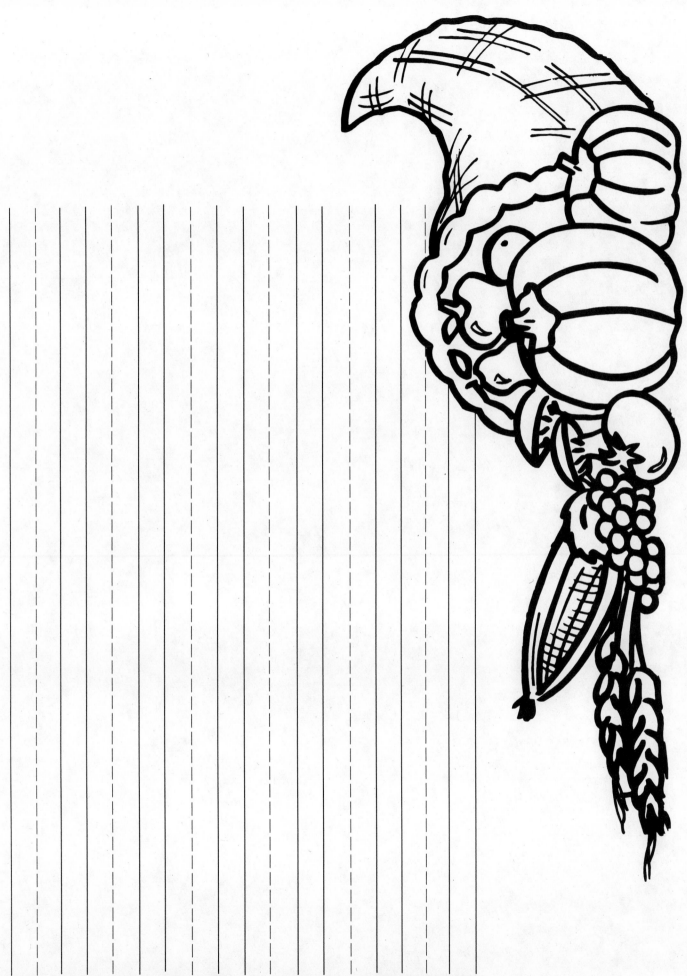

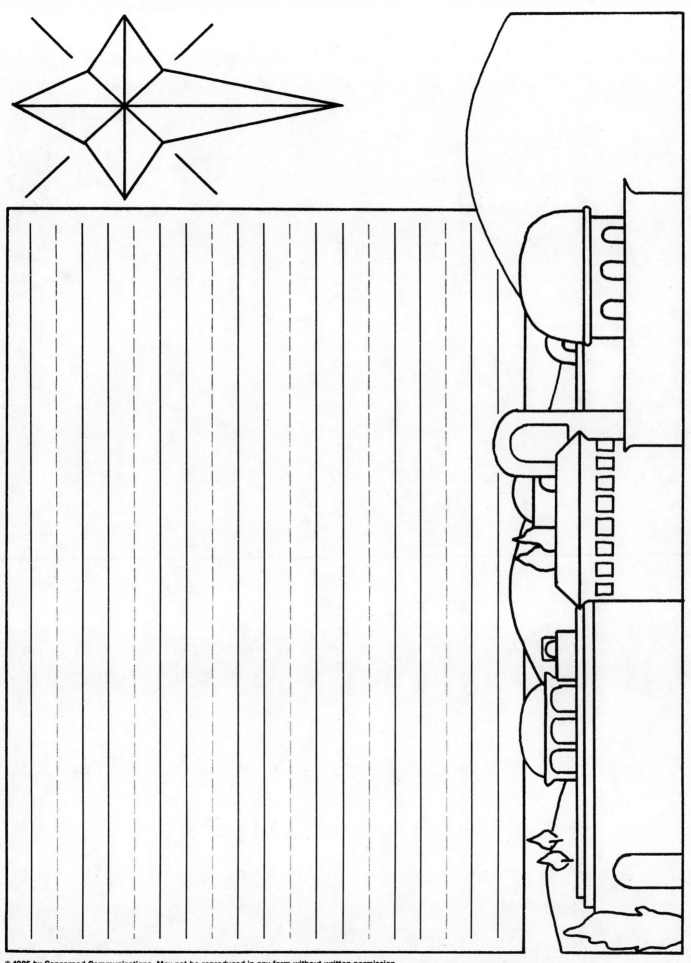

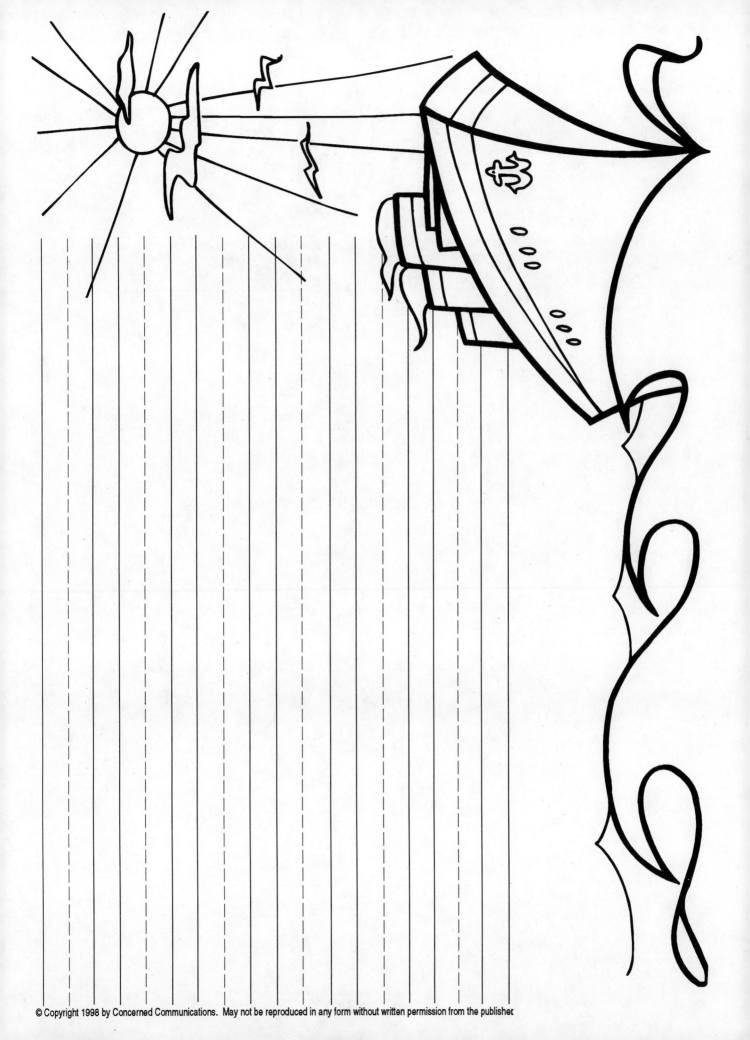

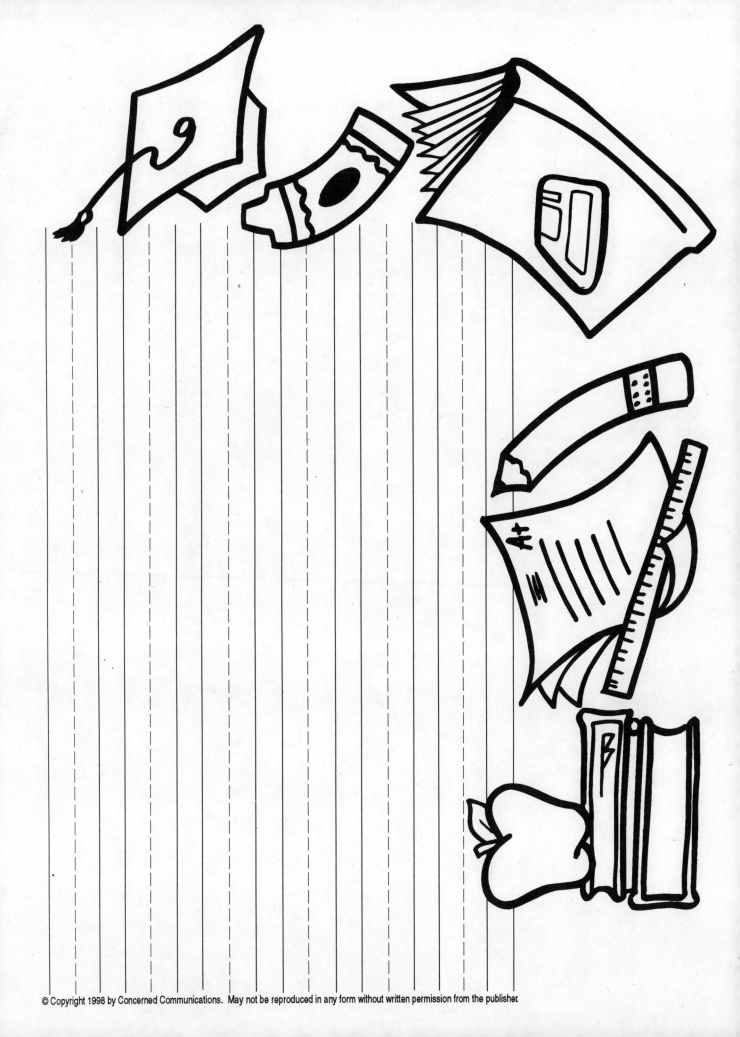